CURRENCY
PROFIT

CURRENCY

PROFIT

QUICK & EASY TRADE SECRETS

Nehemiah M. Douglass

TABLE OF CONTENTS

Chapter 5

Introduction

The Instagram Story And $3,000 Per Day

Honestly, I doubt you and I are very different. Sure, if you picked up this book you most likely have not seen the success you'd like to see as a trader, or you may be trying to enter the world of pips, percentages, and profits, but the reason I say that we probably aren't very different is because chances are, our stories began the same way.

I was a normal 23-year-old college dropout working for an investment management firm. The only reason I even got the job was because of my Microsoft Excel experience that I highlighted on my resume. Luckily, they didn't care much about my education.

Like some of you reading this, I considered myself an entrepreneur. I was working my butt off trying to get things off the ground. Working day-in and day-out on my dreams. However, most of the things I tried would fall through or make me lose money.

My journey as an entrepreneur began as an event planner. I lived near my old university and figured it would be a good idea to throw parties and concerts for the local college kids to enjoy. Things went well for a while until I was forced to move forward.

For my next venture, I launched a mobile app after working overtime for 3 months to afford it. The app saw some decent success, obtaining over 6,000 downloads in the first 45 days, but it obviously wasn't a money maker.

Finally, I was brought to the beginning of our Forex journey. Now, I plan to spend a few minutes explaining this in detail, but first I want to introduce myself. It was important to explain that I was just like you before I got into this side of things because I want you to know that anything is possible. So, let's dive in.

My name is Nehemiah Douglass, most people just call me "Nemo" for short. I'm a 25-year-old Forex trader, mentor, entrepreneur, and owner of my own Forex trading brokerage (IlluminatedMarkets.com). As I write this book, I have over 1000 students worldwide across 20+ different countries, a combined following of 60,000 people online, two 7-figure earning students and two *dozen* 6-figure earners. I've been featured in Forbes Magazine, Huffington Post, Yahoo Finance, Marketwatch, Seeking Alpha,

FOX, ABC, NBC, CBS, and multiple podcasts and radio shows.

On an average day in early 2015, I went to work expecting to clock in, do my work, and leave like I normally would. I can't remember if it was a Tuesday or Wednesday, but I guess that's pretty irrelevant at this point. My job was to reconcile all of the major institutions like Charles Schwab and Deutsche Bank's assets each day, so the job would be very boring and tedious at times.

In between work, I would sneak onto my phone to check my social media and sometimes make updates. I knew if I ever got caught I would get in trouble, but the tasks were so boring at times I couldn't really help myself.

I was scrolling on Instagram and a post seemed to jump out at me. It was from a person I didn't remember following, but the caption and image grabbed my full attention. It read, "I made $3,000 today from my smartphone."

Now, I don't know about you reading this, but that sure was a bold claim to make to the world. At the time, I was working to fund my mobile app through overtime hours so I knew an extra $3,000 could be a life-changing thing for me. I really just wanted to make some money to fund the projects that I was already working on! I had to figure out what this guy was talking about.

I reached out to him and found out that he was a few years younger than me, which took me by surprise. He explained that he was a Forex trader, and that if I paid him $200, he would help me get set up with an account.

After a few days of debating, I went ahead and made the leap. The stranger helped me setup my first brokerage account and the next thing I knew, I was connected to a trading platform. I was in!

However, that's when the big issue came; I didn't know what the heck I was doing. The guy that helped me didn't really provide trading support, so I was on my own to figure things out. It immediately became my mission to become a successful trader. I knew that if I focused on it as hard as I could, that I could find the freedom I was looking for. Six months later, I put in my resignation notice at work. I was free at last.

CHAPTER 1

Let's Set Some Expectations

To start things off on the right foot, I think we need to start by setting some expectations. If we don't have a goal in mind, we're not working towards anything. I want to set some expectations for you as your mentor so we both know exactly what we're getting ourselves into.

COMMIT

You need to make a commitment right now to give Forex your all for the next 6 months. Nothing worth it happens overnight. You have to really work hard in this business to understand things the way that you need to. Granted, some people will see success very quickly, but that's not an expectation you should put on yourself. If you don't make a million dollars in your first month, it's not the end of the world! If you're one of the many who don't see success right away, you just have to keep going.

THE MORE YOU STUDY THE MORE YOU PROFIT

This is a super important one. Forex is a game that has many perspectives and views. Everyone sees and understands the market differently, and there are a million ways to trade the same thing. You have to find what works for YOU! That means the more you study, the more you profit. Keep things as simple as possible in the beginning by learning a strategy similar to the one on **www.forexfortunefactory.com**, and then start to expand your knowledge from there. The last thing I want is for you to feel stuck!

TAKE RESPONSIBILITY FOR YOUR SUCCESS

From here on out, you are in control of your profits and success. No one else. If you are not seeing success, it is nobody's fault besides your own! There are multiple successful traders out there and you are just as worthy to become one as well. If you can't take responsibility for your trades then you should not be in this industry. There are no miracle trading systems or mentorships out there that don't require work!

KEEP A HUMBLE ATTITUDE

I've come to find that there is a curse upon traders worldwide that brings about the worst parts of a person's ego as soon as they start seeing the success rate they're looking for. You have to stay focused and remain grateful when these things happen to you! We as traders have an "ATM effect" that allows us to look at a chart, place a trade, and print money out of thin air. It's very easy to lose yourself in the money and pips, and it's very easy to feel entitled to only your opinion of the markets. You have to keep in mind that everyone is at a different stage in their journey and there are many ways to trade the same thing. Everything is an opinion!

CHAPTER 2

Things You'll Need To Get Started

Of course, we have some tasks for you to complete before you can get started. I've listed the requirements below and the definitions for each.

Brokerage

A brokerage kind of works like a bank account. I personally bank with Wells Fargo here in America, and when I first opened my account the banker told me I would get a certain amount of interest earned for each year that I keep money in my account. A trading brokerage works very similarly, except on this side of things *you* are the one in control of your interest. If you'd like to grow by 5% or 100% per month, it is completely up to you and how much you study. There are many regulated and non-regulated brokerages all around the world that you can research to find what is best for you. Or, you can apply to work with my personal brokerage, **www.illuminatedmarkets.com**

Trading Capital

Now this requirement is going to be flexible based on your current personal finances. However, you're going to need trading capital no matter which route you take. I recommend to my personal trading students that $500 to $1,000 is perfect as a beginner. It's not a ton of money, but it's large enough to payout satisfactory gains on your account. It's completely possible to start with less, but you have to take note that the profits will be much smaller and can really test your patience as a beginner.

Trading Platform

This is where you'll actually execute your trades. A brokerage account does not make the trades for you, it's just where you will hold all of your trading capital. A trading platform is also where you will analyze all of your trades and read charts. You will need to connect your brokerage account to a trading platform such as Metatrader 4 or XStation. These are the most popular trading platforms that most Forex brokerages will offer. You may find brokerages that have their own custom charting softwares that you can try.

Analyzing Software (Optional)

I'm personally not the biggest fan of doing my analysis on Metatrader or Xstation. Instead, I use web-based applications such as **Tradingview.com** to analyze in a much cleaner fashion. There is a free account option, but I highly recommend upgrading to the pro version for added features!

Leverage

Essentially, leverage is a giant loan from your broker. In reality, the Forex market is the largest market in the entire world with 4 to 6 trillion dollars traded daily. In order for people like you and I to participate in such a large market, we need a lot more capital, and that's where our broker comes into play. They give us a loan and pay back our profits in percentages. So to explain, let's say you have the $1000 recommendation that I gave earlier. This is nowhere near what is needed to trade in the Forex market. Our brokerage will give us a leverage of 1:50 up to 1:1000 in some countries to trade with. This means for every $1 you place into your account, the brokerage will give you $50 to trade with. The higher the leverage you have, the more risk you can take on with your account.

Long & Short Positions (Buying & Selling)

This is how we make money. It's not really something you "need to get" per say, but it's something that's necessary to participate in the Forex market. A long or short position is our "bet" in the market. When we go long (buy), we're placing a bet that the market will go up. When we go short (sell), we're placing a bet that the market will go down. Whenever we're correct about our position before the move actually happens, we make money. If the market goes the opposite way against our bet, then we lose money. Pretty simple right?

Understanding of Lot Sizes

There are three different types of lot sizes. To define what a lot size is, it is the size of the trade that we're placing in the market(your position). This is the actual amount that you're placing on your long or short position. If you place $1000 into your brokerage account, this does not mean you are placing $1000 into the market. Remember, everything is based off of percentages, so when you actually place your trade, you're placing a percentage of the money in your account.

The three types of lot sizes:

- Micro = .01 = $0.10 Cents/ Pip
- Mini = .10 = $1.00 / Pip
- Standard = 1.00 = $10.00 / Pip

Here's a scenario. If you place a winning trade in the market that moves 50 pips (we'll get into pips soon), and you have one standard lot, you will calculate $10 x 50 = $500 profit. If you have ten standard lots then you will calculate $100 x 50 = $5,000 profit.

Counting Pips

This is the most important thing of trading. PIPS stands for "Percentage in Point." Pips combined with lot sizes are how we make money each and every week. If you master pips, then you can master the Forex market.

Let's say we have EUR/USD at 1.34273. This number is the exchange rate that EUR can be transferred to USD. In school, we're taught to read text from left to right, but with numbers we read from right to left. Starting with the '3' of the number above, this is called a PIPETTE. These move so quickly that they're almost irrelevant.

Next on our list we have the '7', this is the beginning of our pips. If this 7 moves up to 8, then the market just moved up by 1 pip. If the 7 moves down to 6, then the market just moved down by 1 pip. It's very simple!

However, it becomes even easier when you look at the '2' to the left of it. Let's just say we have 27 now. If this 27 moves to 30, then we know the market just moved 3 pips. If this 27 moves down to 16, then we know the market just moved down by 11 pips.

Most currency pairs will have either 3 or 5 places after the decimal point. You'll usually see 3 places on the Japanese pairs.

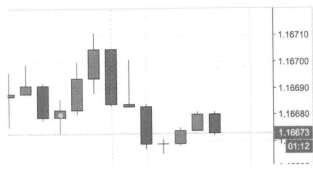

CHAPTER 3

Foundation Fortunes – Meet The Players Of The Game

I had the pleasure of meeting a new contact for dinner in London who had taken interest in me based on my background as a trader. I will not reveal her identity out of respect for her privacy and mine, but there's this thing called fate that is absolutely mind-blowing to me. Over the course of a few hours in a popular gastropub named 'The Ivy,' we shared general world views. I uncovered that she happened to work for a large bank. In my view, that makes her someone who actually moves the forex market that we're discussing . It was just such a rare and in-depth conversation on perspectives that I simply had to share the learnings with you all.

"My Market Maker friend would say there are six levels of participants in the Forex market."

1. **Dealers:** People like my friend, the Market Maker. She makes the market and sets the quote for everyone else below her. She's also out to take everyone below her's money.
2. **Sovereign names:** AKA central banks
3. **Large speculators:** Mostly hedge funds
4. **Commercials:** Business or corporate entities
5. **Real Money Traders:** People who use money to make money without leverage. Mutual fund managers, as an example.
6. **Average Joe/Retails Traders:** The bottom of the food chain. Trades

reactively using profit/loss thresholds.

How the Game is Played - *Understanding Liquidity*

Liquidity is basically the movement of money. Imagine money as water. Liquidity is like water in its *liquid* state, flowing quickly from place to place. Non-liquid funds can be imagined as water in its frozen state or as financial ice cubes. Water is always water, but you have to wait for the ice to melt before the water flows. For example, borrowed money from a loan is still money, but it takes time to process.

Most traders place pending orders; buy limits (bids) and sell limits (offers). These can be defined as orders that have a predetermined entry, or the area where ice cubes are waiting to be melted. Market

Makers use pending orders to project the amount of liquidity available in the market, and move the market strategically to melt these ice cubes and take the traders equity.

(Take a look at the diagram below for an idea of pending orders.)

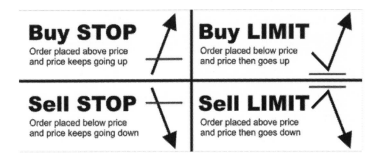

Your Opponent's Dirty Little Secret

Market Makers can see where you've placed these limits, so they know what the majority is hoping for in the market. They know our price point and they know we are betting on a rise or drop in price. Let's say $100 million in buy limits are waiting to make a move. Market Makers want to cause some movement and activate those trades so that they can drop the market the opposite way, ultimately collecting profit. They move the market with their money and make profit from OUR money.

The question becomes, "How am I supposed to win at poker when my opponent is staring directly at my cards?" Simply put, understanding what drives their decisions shifts the game from mission impossible, to potentially profitable calculated risk.

Beating Them at Their Own Game

Life is all about perspective. What the majority is predicting, Market Makers will drive against. Market Makers create certain things on the chart and wait for us to act upon it. They know market drops scare traders. They also know what causes traders to enter in their positions.

It's really a game of cat and mouse.

All of the rules that are passed down from trader to trader such as technical or fundamental analysis are not to be discounted, but you have to understand that everything we see on the chart was put their strategically. They have created their system to stay at the top of the food chain. We also need to adapt and see the market the way they see it. If we trade in-line with Market Makers, we'll stay in the top 5% of traders. They have certain rules they follow that actually makes their method extremely predictable when looking at it with the correct lense. **Learn to play the waiting game and trust the plan.**

The Actual Game Plan Week-by-Week

You should know that the strategy I use is really nothing new. A theory created by Richard Wyckoff about the accumulation and distribution of institutional orders has actually been circulating among elite traders for over 100 years. See the chart below for visual illustration.

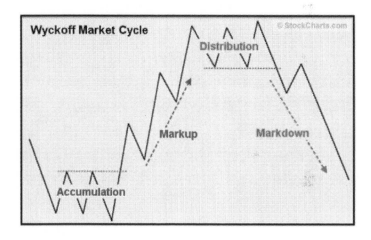

Accumulation or better described as "consolidation" is an extend movement of ups and downs. These are points where market movement hovers more in a lateral motion. The Market Makers hover over these points because this is what forms areas of support and resistance, a popular technical analysis method retail traders use. These areas are usually predictable and move in levels. We'll be covering levels later.

Unfortunately, 95% of traders don't find their way or they lose 40-50% of the time. Learn to anticipate maker behavior the way they have learned to anticipate yours.

Curb Your Fear Response with Knowledge and Logic

Average market movement is around 600 to 1,000 pips per week or 100 to 300 pips per day. That's not to say it will never move more than that, but these are the averages. Market Makers are limited to the amount of movement they can make each week because they are in control of the world economy. Therefore, the market cannot move any one direction for an extended period of time without consequence. Having confidence in this fact changed my game entirely and relieved my fear of the market. What goes up MUST come down.

CHAPTER 4

Identifying Levels – Your Strategy In Action

Levels are crucial to the success of my strategy. If you have read the previous chapters, you'll find this chapter much more in-depth and organized. Level leveraging will break concepts down all the way to the simple basics. I will dive deep into the science behind them and explain what makes them so fundamental as keys to unlocking the full potential of this strategy. My desire is to build your skill in recognizing levels keenly to save you time by avoiding unnecessary struggle and put you in the fast-lane for success.

I encourage you to break out the highlighters and bookmark this chapter because your understanding of levels will determine your success in Forex and in this financial strategy.

What Is A Level?

Most people feel the Forex market is unpredictable, I'd like to say that this is not true. Others may not feel it's unpredictable, but feel they need years and years of practice to develop their skill level. This is also not true for most people. As you probably know, the market has two options. It can go up. It can go down -- either way it can make you money. Both upswings and downswings follow a predictable trend, a three to five level cycle. The cycle can be seen in both short and long-term time frames. There are several views available to you; monthly, weekly, 4-hour and others. For our purposes of identifying levels, I always rely on the hourly and daily charts for the clearest view of what matters most.

Understanding how the market moves in these levels is the simplest way to see the market for what it really is. Psychology of the market is key to success in this business. It's also the way my students and I are able to profit from the Forex market each and every week. To explain further, the market will move up or down for three to five levels. At this point, there is normally a reversal or a trend reset, which we will get into later. When you learn how to catch the proper end of these reversals or resets, it's extremely easy to become a profitable trader.

A level is an area of consolidation. In the last chapter, we covered accumulation periods and accumulation zones, where the market hovers to motivate buyers and sellers and essentially collects contracts. It is more of a controlled zone than a horizontal line. I look for two to four points within a range as diagramed, which I often refer to as "hits." You aren't looking for perfection! You are looking for trends of lateral movement over time. This is the basic concept of a level.

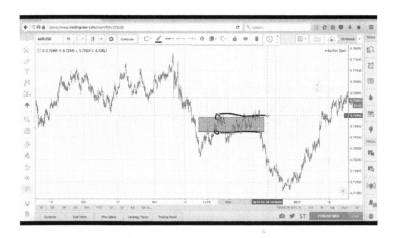

On almost any charting platform, you can set up Exponential Moving Averages (EMAs). EMAs take all the jumpy price movements on the charts of ups and downs and simplifies them into smoothly plotted lines. Using EMAs in your trading strategy can help you to understand where you are in the three to five level cycle.

Important: EMAs are intended as a visual guide and should not distract your attention from actual price movement. They are based on the candle movement and are known to have a lag, coming after the moves have already been made. You CAN use them to help you identify your levels and the behaviors they indicate, but only for simplification.

EMAs can also be used for target profits. The 200 EMA out of a level three is our first target profit and the 800 EMA outside of a level two is our second target profit. If you have the time and patience, you can ride out a long term trade (often referred to as a swing trade) until the next three to five level cycle is complete.

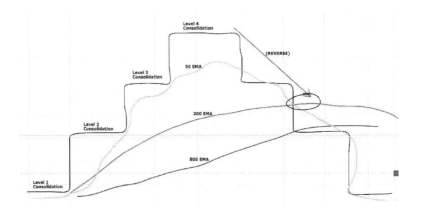

When the market returns to the 200 EMA,
Market Makers have recollected equity
after driving the market up or down to get
people to set their orders. The 200 EMA is
your indicator that their profit target has
been reached. They've recollected equity
by sparking emotion in traders, driving
price one direction and creating a sense of
hope that things won't change by moving
in that one direction. Once there are
enough traders committed, they take the
market the opposite way. Think about the
times you've looked at a chart as an

inexperienced trader. You see a bunch of things going on with the chart, but you also see that the market has been rising almost non-stop for the last few days or even weeks. After checking a few websites, you see that multiple people have been profiting from this exact same rise.

So, what do you do? You obviously don't want to miss the upward move, right? That would be terrible! There's so much money to be made and you have a super mansion to buy next week. You go ahead and open up a buy position, most likely over-leveraged on your position, dreaming of your mansion on the lake and five supercars. A few hours later, you go back to check your platform and realize that the market has dropped 100 points against you. You have no idea what the heck happened, and after checking a few more websites you see that people profited on the move back down as well. The websites you found are saying there will be another rise later on so you hold onto your position instead of closing it, but the market never does come back. It keeps dropping to the point that you're driven into margin trouble and eventually have no more equity in your account. Maybe you should have believed all the people saying the market was unpredictable.

Pretty vivid picture above, right?

I can bet that hundreds (if not thousands) of traders reading this can relate to this exact story in most respects. Unfortunately, 95% of traders fail because they never learn what I'm trying to teach you in this chapter. You have to understand that we are practically at war with these Market Makers. They want our money, and they have all the equity, power, and platforms to make sure this goal happens. I mean, think about it; where do these markets even come from? I sure as heck didn't create them, and I'm guessing you didn't either.

The reason I use the hourly chart is because I want to see levels on an intraday basis. Intraday trades are usually 1 to 5 days. The daily chart also has levels but since it's a higher time frame, it will take longer for the full level to form. Understanding which cycle the daily is in, however, will give you excellent confirmation for the intraday basis. **The market behaves almost the exact same way on every chart.**

An actual trend reversal is when you see a rise of three to five levels that is followed by an equal and mirroring fall. A trend reset is when a rising market begins to fall, but turns on its heel and quickly starts climbing back up in value.

CHAPTER 5

Conclusion

The life of a Forex trader doesn't have to be short-lived. You CAN succeed in this market with the right tools. It's important that you understand what is possible for you.

I want you to stay encouraged and trust your journey. There is always light at the other end of the tunnel if you just keep going. Forex trading can be one of the most difficult businesses to be in, but also one of the most rewarding. Every trader's journey will be different, but they will all start out the same.

When I first started my journey, I lost 5 different deposits into my brokerage and felt completely defeated. I had little to no money after my monthly bills, and losing my investments was very difficult for me. Trading can bring out so many emotions that it's hard to stay balanced.

Stick to your trading plan...

Going against the grain of your trading plan can be extremely costly. When you win trades, learn to step away and sit on your hands. Don't force trades out of false confidence. Another important thing to remember is not to let losses hold you down for too long. It's going to hurt, but you have to remember that it's only temporary. Don't let the pain of loss make you question your strategy.

For those that are ready to take things to the next level, I have an opportunity for you that I don't think you want to miss. I want to give you the opportunity to work with me personally and receive my training videos. All you have to do is head over to

www.forexfortunefactory.com to register for my training.

You will get the above strategy broken down to you in detail, with hours of content readily available to you.

Made in the USA
Columbia, SC
27 January 2018